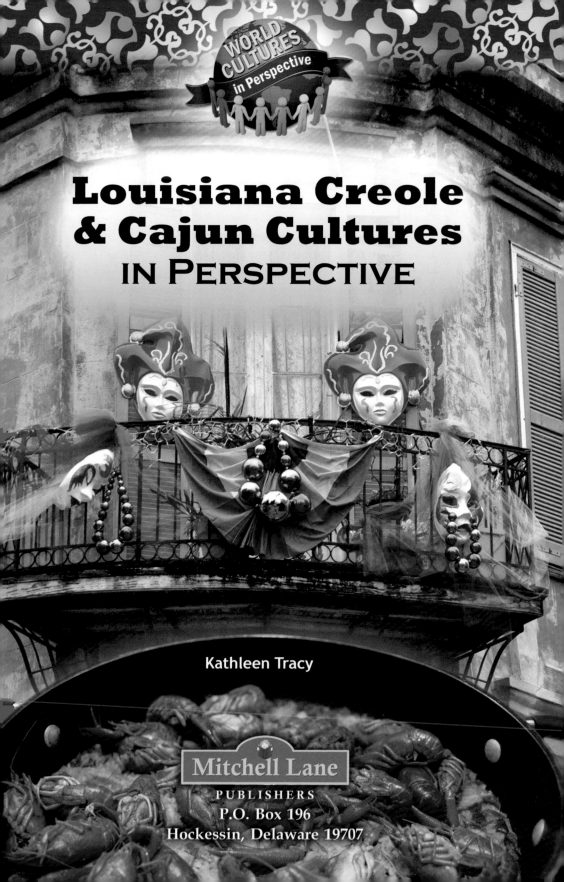

WORLD CULTURES in Perspective

Louisiana Creole & Cajun Cultures
IN PERSPECTIVE

Kathleen Tracy

Mitchell Lane
PUBLISHERS
P.O. Box 196
Hockessin, Delaware 19707

Brazilian Cultures IN PERSPECTIVE

Caribbean Cultures IN PERSPECTIVE

East Asian Cultures IN PERSPECTIVE

Islamic Culture IN PERSPECTIVE

Israeli Culture IN PERSPECTIVE

Louisiana Creole & Cajun Cultures IN PERSPECTIVE

Native Alaskan Cultures IN PERSPECTIVE

North African Cultures IN PERSPECTIVE

Polynesian Cultures IN PERSPECTIVE

Southeast Asian Cultures IN PERSPECTIVE

Mitchell Lane
PUBLISHERS

Printing   1   2   3   4   5   6   7   8   9

Library of Congress Cataloging-in-Publication Data
Tracy, Kathleen.
 Louisiana Creole and Cajun cultures in perspective / by Kathleen Tracy.
     pages cm. — (World cultures in perspective)
 Includes bibliographical references and index.
 ISBN 978-1-61228-562-7 (library bound)
 1. Cajuns—Louisiana—Social life and customs—Juvenile literature.
 2. Creoles—Louisiana—Social life and customs—Juvenile literature.
 3. Louisiana—Social life and customs—Juvenile literature. 4. Louisiana—Civilization—Juvenile literature. I. Title.
 F380.A2T73 2014
 305.84'10763—dc23

                                                            2014009364

eBook ISBN: 9781612286013

PUBLISHER'S NOTE: This story is based on the author's extensive research, which she believes to be accurate. Documentation of this research is on pages 60–61.

The Internet sites referenced herein were active as of the publication date. Due to the fleeting nature of some web sites, we cannot guarantee they will all be active when you are reading this book.

To reflect current usage, we have chosen to use the secular era designations BCE ("before the common era") and CE ("of the common era") instead of the traditional designations BC ("before Christ") and AD (*anno Domini,* "in the year of the Lord").

                                                            PBP

CONTENTS

Introduction: A Cultural Melting Pot 6

Chapter 1: THE LOUISIANA PURCHASE............................ 8

   Manifest Destiny 14

Chapter 2: THE EVOLUTION OF THE CAJUNS..................16

   Cajun Agriculture...22

Chapter 3: THE CREOLES...24

   The Haiti Connection 30

Chapter 4: TRADITIONS...32

   Faubourg Tremé..40

Chapter 5: RELIGIOUS TRADITIONS 42

   Voodoo 46

Chapter 6: NOTABLE CAJUNS AND CREOLES..................48

Map of Louisiana...55

Experiencing Cajun and Creole Culture 56

Timeline..58

Chapter Notes 59

Further Reading 60

   Books...60

   Works Consulted 60

Glossary..62

Index..63

INTRODUCTION
A Cultural Melting Pot

French explorers. Cajuns. Spanish aristocrats. Creoles. The bayou. Gumbo. Pirates. Political corruption. Jazz. Voodoo. Mardi Gras.

Louisiana's colorful past has shaped the state's culturally diverse present. Its territory has had numerous claimants. The first was explorer Hernando de Soto on behalf of Spain in 1541, followed by Robert de la Salle of France and even the short-lived Republic of West Florida before it became the 18th state to join the Union in 1812. At the start of the Civil War, Louisiana became an independent republic for two weeks after seceding from the Union before joining the Confederacy.

And hardly any people have influenced the culture of Louisiana as much as the Creoles and Cajuns, two groups whose customs inform almost everything from the local cuisine and music to the region's unique funeral traditions. A Cajun is someone whose ancestors came from Acadia, a region in what is now the Canadian Maritime provinces: Prince Edward Island, Nova Scotia, and New Brunswick. Creoles include the descendants of people originally from Europe, Africa, and the Caribbean.

Both Creoles and Cajuns have been strongly influenced by French culture—Louisiana is the only state that bases its laws on the Napoleonic Code of the early nineteenth century—but there are distinct historical, linguistic, geographical, and ethnic differences between the two. However, over time the Creole and Cajun cultures have become increasingly intermingled, and some experts suggest the two groups are evolving to create a new blended group that is uniquely Louisianan.

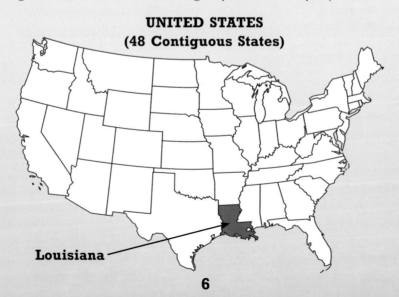

UNITED STATES
(48 Contiguous States)

Louisiana

Southern Louisiana bayou

CHAPTER ONE
The Louisiana Purchase

New Orleans,
early 1800s

It was one of the biggest real estate deals in history, doubling the size of the United States with the stroke of a pen in 1803. But at the time what was known as the Louisiana Purchase was a controversial, hot-button issue that polarized Congress and the public over whether or not the young country should actively expand its territory. In the end, the Louisiana Territory proved too important for President Thomas Jefferson to ignore.

After Britain successfully gained a foothold on the North American continent along the Atlantic coast during the seventeenth century, the French established themselves further inland. Explorer Robert de la Salle went to Canada in 1666 and set up a fur trading post. He befriended the local Iroquois Indians, who told him of a mighty river that led to an ocean. Like many explorers of the time, he was obsessed with finding new routes to the Far East, and in 1682 he became the first European to sail down the Mississippi River to the Gulf of Mexico.

He claimed the Mississippi River Basin for France and called it the Louisiana Territory, in honor of King Louis XIV. Two years later la Salle led an expedition that included would-be settlers but they got lost and lost all four of their ships. La Salle's harsh leadership style angered his men, who eventually killed him.

In 1699, French officials asked noted explorer Pierre d'Iberville to help settle the area. He established a settlement in what is now Mississippi. His brother Jean-Baptiste de Bienville founded New Orleans in 1718. Slowly, the population grew over the next several decades, with most people living in and around a few towns

Robert de la Salle (1643–1687)

such as New Orleans. But by the mid-eighteenth century France was largely ignoring the colony. Near the end of the French and Indian War in 1763, France signed a treaty that gave Spain the entire Louisiana territory west of the Mississippi River.

In November 1799, Napoleon Bonaparte staged a coup d'état in France and established himself as the country's leader. As soon as he came to power, Napoleon wanted to re-establish the French empire in North America. In 1800, Spain agreed to return Louisiana to France. President Thomas Jefferson had always considered France as a friend and ally. But he saw a serious potential problem after the Spanish authorities, still officiating on behalf of the French, revoked a treaty that granted Americans the right to store goods in New Orleans. The United States depended on New Orleans for its economic survival. Allowing France to control the port could be financially disastrous for the new country.

In February 1803, Congress debated whether Jefferson should use military force to enforce the country's rights to the Mississippi and eventually authorized him to organize a militia of 80,000

**Napoleon Bonaparte,
shown here in 1802**

soldiers to protect American interests on the Mississippi. While Congress might have been ready to go to war, Jefferson was committed to diplomacy first. He named James Monroe to be his special envoy to France. Monroe, along with Ambassador Robert Livingston, hoped to buy the relatively small portion of the Louisiana territory east of the Mississippi or perhaps just New Orleans. At the very least they needed to maintain American access to the Mississippi River. Jefferson authorized them to offer up to $10 million.

The timing of the negotiations turned out to be in the Americans' favor. France was embroiled in a slave rebellion in Haiti and on the brink of war with Britain. Napoleon was strapped financially. His passion to re-establish a French empire in North America had cooled. Instead, France offered to sell the entire Louisiana territory—more than 828,000 square miles from New Orleans to the Rocky Mountains—to the United States for $15 million. Even though that sum was beyond their budget and the purchase itself was beyond what Jefferson had instructed them to do, Monroe and

Livingston negotiated a purchase treaty and signed it on April 30, 1803. Jefferson made the announcement on July 4, 1803, the 27th anniversary of the Declaration of Independence. However, the Louisiana Purchase would not be official until the Senate gave its approval to the treaty, the House of Representatives agreed to provide the necessary funding, and it was all signed by Jefferson.

Acquiring the Louisiana territory had an obvious tremendous upside, but there were questions over whether the purchase was constitutional. Jefferson had always been very vocal that the federal government's constitutional powers should be strictly interpreted. Article IV of the Constitution said that new states could be added. But it did not specifically say that the government could buy foreign territories.

He wrote, "The General Government has no powers but such as the Constitution gives it . . . it has not given it power of holding foreign territory, and still less of incorporating it into the Union. An amendment of the Constitution seems necessary for this."[1] He even

States and Territories of the United States, April 30, 1803

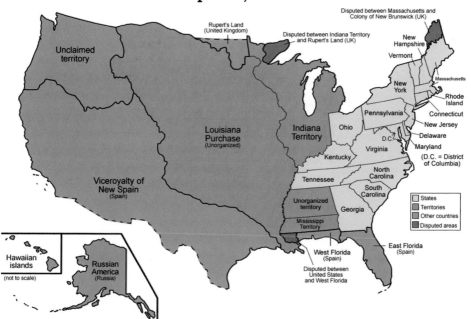

went so far as to draft an amendment to authorize the purchase of Louisiana retroactively.

Congress felt that the proposed amendment was unnecessary, and the Senate passed "An act to enable the President of the United States to take possession of the territories ceded by France to the United States, by the treaty concluded at Paris on the thirtieth of April last, and for the temporary government thereof."[2] Jefferson signed the Act five days later. France officially turned New Orleans and the rest of the territory over to the United States on December 20, 1803.

Even though Jefferson may have bent his belief on how the Constitution should be interpreted, he recognized the importance of the Louisiana Purchase. He later noted, "It is incumbent on those who accept great charges to risk themselves on great occasions."[3]

Jefferson doubled the size of the United States—at a cost of less than three cents an acre—and set a precedent for acquiring new lands through peaceful means. But there was a question over the exact southern and western boundaries, which were not defined in the purchase. This led to a new era of exploration and the eventual settling of the west. It also led to a new influx of settlers to Louisiana, who would form the foundation for the arrival of the Cajuns and the Creoles.

Jefferson signing the Louisiana Purchase

The Louisiana Purchase made New Orleans part of the United States. Swedish-born artist Thure de Thulstrup (1848–1930) depicts the first raising of the American flag in New Orleans on March 10, 1804.

Manifest Destiny

The Louisiana Territory stretched from the Mississippi River in the east to the Rocky Mountains in the west, the Gulf of Mexico in the south, and the Canadian border in the north. Part or all of 15 states were eventually created from the land, including Louisiana, which was admitted into the Union as the 18th state in 1812.

The Louisiana Purchase was the foundation for what became known as Manifest Destiny. This is the belief that Americans were destined—some felt it was God's will—to ultimately control North America from sea to shining sea.

The term Manifest Destiny was first used in 1845 by newspaper editor John O'Sullivan in an article about the proposed annexation of Texas. O'Sullivan stated that it was America's "manifest destiny to overspread the continent allotted by Providence for the free development of our yearly multiplying millions."[4] O'Sullivan argued that expansion would make the United States a political and social superpower and believed it was not only the country's destiny but also its responsibility to tame the wilderness and establish civilization.

Manifest Destiny was never an official governmental policy. But its spirit prompted passage in 1862 of the Homestead Act, which gave settlers in the western territories plots of land at little or no cost. The wide-open spaces of the west appealed to many Americans' sense of adventure, which led to additional land acquisition beyond the Louisiana territory and a further age of exploration and settlement.

Emigrants heading to the lands of the
Louisiana Purchase to establish new homes

CHAPTER TWO
The Evolution of the Cajuns

This painting depicts the forced expulsion of the Acadians in 1755.

According to the United States census, the population of Louisiana in 1820 was a little more than 143,000.[1] Among those were approximately 4,000 residents of French heritage who had come to the American South by way of Canada. Eventually known as Cajuns, they were united by a common language, a common ancestry, a shared culture, and a shared history of persecution.

The Louisiana Cajuns trace their history back to early 17th century France, in a western region called the Vendée that lies along the Atlantic Coast. Starting in 1604, people from that area immigrated to Canada and settled primarily in what is now Nova Scotia as well as nearby areas. The land was so fertile that the settlers called it Acadia, or heaven on earth. The small settlements of the first colonists grew into prosperous farms and trading posts.

At Acadia's peak, there were 15,000 residents. The original French settlers had spoken a regional dialect, which evolved essentially into its own language, also called Acadian. After several generations, the Acadians had developed a culture that was

The Vendée region of France.

distinctly their own. Acadia was mostly ignored by the French kings, who were more focused on the region around the province of Quebec. And the British were putting their resources into their New England colonies. Even so, control of Acadia went back and forth between England and France several times. Many Acadians tried to avoid picking sides and became known as the "French neutrals." That strategy worked for a long time, allowing them to live quietly and prosper.

After Great Britain acquired permanent control of Acadia in 1710, increasing tensions led to numerous conflicts between the two sides. Eventually the British wanted to establish their sovereignty in Canada and colonize the area with British subjects. After a century and a half of building a thriving community, the Acadians' idyllic life came to an abrupt end in 1755. Charles Lawrence, the governor of Nova Scotia, demanded that Acadian men sign a loyalty oath to English King George II and denounce their Catholic religion. When the men refused, they were arrested.

Lawrence wrote a deportation order that expelled the Acadians from their land. Within days, their farms, churches, and shops were burned down by British soldiers. Their crops were destroyed and their livestock slaughtered.

Some families were separated as men and younger males were jailed and the women put onto British ships. Many Acadians went to other British colonies. Younger Acadians were made servants to farmers in Massachusetts, New York, and Pennsylvania. In the Carolina colonies, local officials tried to take Acadian children away from their parents to work on plantations. Others were sent back to Europe, primarily to England and France. Those who returned to France were treated as outcasts.

Portrait of King George II of England

As Yale history professor John Mack Faragher notes, "The operation carried out by Anglo-American forces in 1755 included the forced deportation of civilian populations, the cruel and inhumane treatment of prisoners, and the plunder and wanton destruction of communities, practices now defined as 'crimes against humanity' and 'ethnic cleansing.'"[2]

This was just the start. The British launched additional "cleansing" campaigns in the following years. These deportations were often dangerous. In 1758, a ship called the *Duke William* carrying hundreds of Acadians sank in the North Atlantic. More than 360 people perished. In all, some historians estimate that close to fifty percent of Acadians died as a direct consequence of their expulsion from Canada.

Eventually some Acadians made their way to Louisiana, with the first group arriving in 1765. The governor welcomed the Acadians, mostly to help minimize British influence. Author Carl Brasseaux explains that "The acting governor, Charles Philippe Aubry, was familiar with their plight, since he had encountered the Acadians a few years earlier when in New England. He planned to put them on the right bank of the Mississippi River close to New Orleans. But the area he chose was covered with hardwood forests and was susceptible to flooding. Clearing the land and building levees would not allow them to begin farming. So he allowed them to go to the Attakapas region."[3]

Afterward, other Acadians who had originally been taken to the French West Indies and Maryland also made their way to Louisiana. These transplants set up small settlements, mostly in the uninhabited bayous and prairies spread over 22 parishes, the name Louisiana gives to counties.

In 1785, a fleet of seven ships brought 2,000 Acadians to Louisiana from France. Spain had assumed the expenses, since it wanted settlers in the land to protect against a possible British invasion. Once in Louisiana the Acadians were given the choice of where to go. A majority of earlier Acadian settlers had taken the land along the Mississippi River, so most of this group decided to go to the bayous, areas of slow-moving water or wetlands.

A bayou in Louisiana. Bayou comes from _bayuk_, a Choctaw Indian word for _small stream._

After Etienne de Boré successfully produced the first granulated sugar in Louisiana in 1795, it prompted a rush of planters growing sugar cane. The industry provided jobs for many Cajuns, such as this farmer with his daughter.

In all, nearly 4,000 Acadians relocated to Louisiana. Having to start over with no land of their own and few possessions, they took the menial jobs others didn't want. They remained mostly poor, supporting themselves by growing their own crops and raising their own livestock. They remained a close-knit community, united by their common language and culture and by the fact that they were clearly considered outsiders by other Louisianans. They rarely married outside their communities and suffered the second-class citizen status new immigrants have historically experienced in the United States, from the Irish and Italians in the 19th and 20th centuries to Hispanics in more recent decades.

After the Civil War the South struggled to rebuild and overcome the economic devastation it suffered in its losing cause. With so many people poor and struggling, the humble living conditions of the Acadians seemed somewhat commonplace. Slowly, they started marrying non-Acadians, who often learned to speak Acadian French. Now they became known as the Cajuns, from the way in which people quickly pronounced "Acadian." Rather than saying uh-CAY-dee-un, they simply said CAY-dzhun. As they grew in number their traditions and culture began to dominate many areas of life in Louisiana. Even so, they also suffered prejudice, such as efforts to outlaw the speaking of Cajun French in schools—even in those attended only by Cajun children.

The next significant social change occurred in the aftermath of World War II. Many Cajun service veterans had seen a much wider world during their service. That prompted the traditionally insular Cajun community to spread out, with more individuals moving away from small, exclusively French-speaking communities into the mainstream of Louisiana life.

In other words, slowly and steadily the Acadians became Americanized, though their culture would continue to be known as Cajun. Despite the increasingly diverse blood-lines, their culture survived into the 21st century.

Cajun Agriculture

During their time in Canada, the Acadians excelled as farmers, and they brought those skills to Louisiana. The Acadians who settled in the bayou areas mostly raised livestock, while the communities along the Mississippi River grew crops. However, the different soil and warmer climate meant that they needed to learn how to produce new types of food. Instead of crops such as the vegetables, oats, rye, barley, flax, and wheat that had been the staples of their Canadian farms, in Louisiana they focused on corn, cotton, rice, and tobacco. Most of them also maintained small gardens of primarily peas and beans for personal consumption. Their orchards of apple trees in Arcadia gave way to peach and fig trees in Louisiana.

Before they could plant, the Acadians had to prepare the land by clearing forests and building levees to keep out floodwaters from the Mississippi River in times of heavy rains. They also had to develop new techniques of planting. In Acadia, farmers sowed seeds by hand, then covered them with a bit of dirt. But it rains a lot in Louisiana, which would have washed the seeds away. So the Cajuns had to plow their fields, meaning that they needed oxen to pull their plows. The Acadians on the prairie land typically raised chickens, cows, and pigs.

The average Acadian in Louisiana only grew enough crops to earn enough money to buy items they couldn't grow or make themselves. So even though they were poor, they managed to have enough to eat and maintained the bare essentials of life.

A Cajun farm

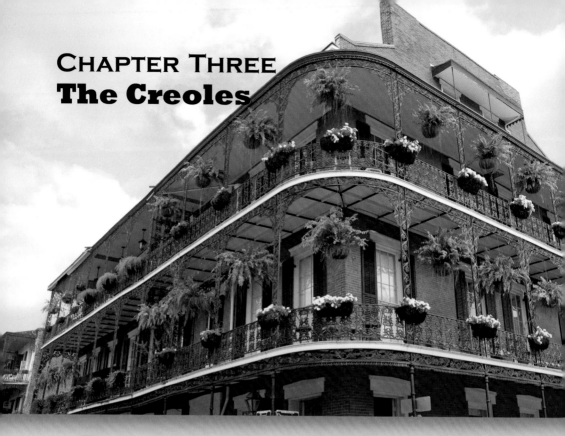

CHAPTER THREE
The Creoles

 Unlike the Cajuns, who have a distinct ethnic lineage, Creoles are racially and ethnically diverse and did not migrate from a single area.

The term "Creole" is derived from the Portuguese word *crioulo*, which referred to a slave born and raised in his or her master's household, rather than being imported. It was later expanded to identify descendants of French, Spanish, or Portuguese settlers living in the West Indies and Latin America. In the United States "Creole" was officially defined in the early 1700s as a child born in Louisiana, rather than in France or Spain. Their ancestors were upper-class whites, many of whom were plantation owners or officials during the French and Spanish colonial periods.

Whites of mixed French/Spanish heritage identified themselves as French Creoles and were all Catholic. The white French Creoles spoke what became known as Colonial French, which developed into its own specific dialect. Generally, Creoles married only other Creoles.

St. Louis Cathedral in New Orleans is named for French King Louis IX, who was canonized as a saint in 1297. It has long been the scene of weddings involving Creoles.

The definition of Creole became a legal classification after the United States took control of Louisiana in 1803. At the time Creoles included the Spanish aristocrats, who had ruled New Orleans and Louisiana from the mid-1700s until the early 1800s. Even so, French language and social customs remained dominant under Spanish rule.

However, Americans began to refer to African slaves who were born in the colony as Creoles. That was a way of distinguishing them from new arrivals from Africa. Over time, the black Creoles and Africans developed a French-West African hybrid language called Creole French or Louisiana Creole French. It is still spoken today in central Louisiana but hardly ever in New Orleans.

In Louisiana's early colonial years, there were not many European women so French settlers and officials frequently had relationships with African women. Even when more European women moved to Louisiana, wealthy white Creole men still took women of color as their mistresses, both before and after their marriages. These arrangements were known as plaçages. They often included a promise by the man to grant freedom to his mistress if she was a slave and to provide for any children they had together.

The specific meaning of Louisiana Creole came to mean free people of color: mixed-race individuals who were concentrated in southern Louisiana and New Orleans. This group was also formed during the territory's French and Spanish rule. It was comprised initially of children born of colonial men and female slaves, who were mostly African but could be Caribbean as well.

So three general groups composed Creole society: whites of European origin and mixed-race Creoles who were educated and often wealthy made up the highest class; free blacks, emancipated slaves, and their descendants made up the middle class; and household slaves were the lowest class. But all Creoles, no matter what their social class, looked down on Americans who were settling in Louisiana in ever-increasing numbers.

Creoles who were free people of color during French and Spanish rule formed a distinct social class. Many were educated and became wealthy property owners or businessmen. They were also politically active. Especially in New Orleans, persons of color were wealthier, more secure and more established than blacks elsewhere in Louisiana. While under Spanish and French rule this was not a problem.

The situation changed with the arrival of Americans from New England and other states after the Louisiana Purchase. The cultural diversity, out-in-the-open racial intermingling, and acceptance of African traditions of the slave class of Louisiana in general and New Orleans in particular shocked and offended some of the newly arrived Americans, especially Southerners. They pressured Louisiana's first US-appointed governor, W.C.C. Claiborne, to change them.

Claiborne responded by trying to make English the official language. But French Creoles responded with outrage and protested. Creoles of both white ancestry and free people of color also resisted attempts to segregate the population.

Quickly realizing he needed local support to make any changes, Claiborne backed down and restored French as an official language. New Orleans became a city divided between Creoles and Americans.

William Charles Claiborne (1775–1817) was Louisiana's first governor. He was later selected as a US senator for the state in March 1817, but served just eight months until his death that November.

CHAPTER THREE

The Creoles lived east of a wide boulevard named Canal Street, in what is now known as the French Quarter. American migrants settled to the west. As an increasing number of people from other parts of the country moved to the area, the locals identified themselves as French Creoles to distinguish themselves from the new arrivals.

While the Civil War gave hope to southern slaves, it made Louisiana's free persons of color nervous. Even though slaves were emancipated and were now freemen and women, the South's response was to immediately develop a segregated society. Louisiana's three-tiered Creole society was gradually diluted and endangered by large numbers of Americans who believed the races should be separate and unequal. By the 1880s, the growing number

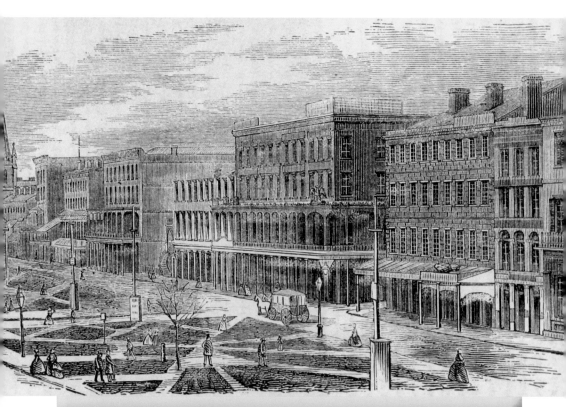

Canal Street has been one of New Orleans' main thoroughfares since the mid-nineteenth century.

of English-speaking Americans in New Orleans and Louisiana caused the decline in French as an official language.

A century later, Creoles largely ceased to exist as a distinct group. Today the identification of a Creole is loosely applied. Creole identity is characterized by the French language and social customs—especially cuisine—regardless of racial makeup. Many young Creoles of color today identify themselves as African Americans.

Louisiana historian Fred B. Kniffen believes the term Creole "has been loosely extended to include people of mixed blood, a dialect of French, a breed of ponies, a distinctive way of cooking, a type of house, and many other things. It is therefore no precise term and should not be defined as such."[1]

While Creole society may no longer be an easily identifiable group or community, the culture's influence remains readily visible to anyone visiting New Orleans or southern Louisiana.

Goods were transported on the Mississippi for many years using steamboats. This photo, taken about 1900, shows several of them along the levee in New Orleans.

The Haiti Connection

Many Louisiana Creoles were descendants of French settlers who originated in the colony of Saint-Domingue on the Caribbean island of Hispaniola. With nearly half a million slaves to work its sugar and coffee plantations, Saint-Domingue became very profitable even though the slaves worked under especially harsh conditions. In the wake of the French Revolution in 1789, the ideals of freedom spread to the colony. Two years later, the slaves rose in open revolt. Many white and mixed-race slave owners who were living on the island were either killed or fled. Some of the refugees came to New Orleans.

Black Haitian rebels attack French troops in September 1802. Sixteen months later Haiti became the first independent nation in Latin America.

Toussaint L'Ouverture (1743–1803), a self-educated slave, was one of the leaders of the revolution. He took control of the Spanish portion of Hispaniola in 1801, resulting in more refugees. Some of the new exiles headed straight to Louisiana. Others went to Cuba first and then ended up in New Orleans. By 1815, a total of more than 11,000 refugees had settled in New Orleans, doubling the city's population. The influx also further diversified the Creole population.

The slave rebellion went on for more than a decade and finally ended in November 1803 when the rebels defeated the French at the Battle of Vertières. After that, the former slaves established an independent country on January 1, 1804 and named it Haiti. It was the second independent nation in the Americas.

The Haitian Revolution was the only slave revolt to result in the founding of a new country and marked a turning point in European attitudes towards New World colonialism.

Toussaint l'Ouverture

Traditions

While Cajun and Creole cultures have very different histories and backgrounds, they share a common link in their French origins. Because they ended up living literally next to each other, there has been some overlap over time with each group influencing the other. Individually and collectively, they have exerted a tremendous influence in every area of culture, especially in the arts.

Early Acadian music centered around the violin and ancient French folk dances passed down through generations. After settling in Louisiana, Cajuns incorporated the accordions which were popular in German music, as well as African influences represented in jazz and the blues. Black Creole zydeco music developed in a similar way, relying strongly on the violin and accordion but more noticeably integrating characteristics of Caribbean music.

Dancing is also an important cultural expression. When New Orleans was under French and Spanish rule, Creoles held weekly public balls, particularly on Saturday nights. These formal dances were particularly popular with the white Creoles, although wealthy

Creoles of color also attended. The balls—which regularly lasted all night—were social events for all ages, a time for young people to meet and flirt and for adults to play cards and gossip.

Perhaps the most identifiable cultural aspect for both Cajun and Creole cultures is food. Broadly speaking, Cajun cooking is often viewed as being more "country," while Creole cooking is regarded as more sophisticated or "citified." It is a blend of a variety of New Orleans cultures including Italian, Spanish, African, German, Caribbean, Native American, and Portuguese. Another difference is that Cajun meals were flavorful but functional, made by a family member, while many Creoles employed chefs. As a general rule, Creole cuisine has a bit more variety because of the easier access Creoles had to exotic ingredients.

Cajun food developed from local ingredients and the Cajuns' modest way of life. Meals tended to be cooked in single pots and incorporated a variety of ingredients. Cajun cooking is likely to use pork, chicken, and sausage. Cooks often include crawfish as well. Many dishes use rice either as a side dish or as part of the main entrée. Popular dishes include étouffée (a stew made with crawfish),

Crawfish étouffée

boudin and andouille sausage, and jambalaya, which is similar to Spanish paella (another stew-like meal).

Creole dishes usually move toward lighter options, such as crab, shrimp and oysters. This difference is especially noticeable in traditional gumbos.

Cajun and Creole recipes often call for bell peppers, celery, and onions. Creole dishes include tomatoes, mustard, allspice, okra, and garlic while Cajun food often features cayenne pepper and other spicy ingredients like thyme, paprika, pepper, and filé (ground sassafras root).

Jambalaya was created in Louisiana and is a variation of Spanish paella. It is often made with one or more meats, typically crawfish, chicken, andouille sausage, or shrimp.

Both Creole and Cajun cuisine uses roux, a mixture of flour and cooking fat used to thicken sauces and gravies. Cajuns typically use oil as the fat, while Creoles generally use butter—a reflection that Creoles traditionally had better access to dairy products than Cajuns.

In certain parts of Louisiana, people still speak both Creole and Cajun French. Creole is grammatically distinct from traditional French and has been influenced by Native American and African languages in addition to Spanish. Cajuns speak Acadian French, with the addition of various words from other languages.

Okra

Creole French is considered an endangered language. There are very few people who speak only Creole, and according to estimates no more than 30,000 people know it. Only half that many speak Cajun French. This has prompted organizations, such as the Council for the Development of French in Louisiana, to initiate programs to preserve the two languages.

Creoles had well-defined marriage customs. Young Creole women had to marry before they were 25. When they came of age, potential suitors would come to the family home and visit. After four such visits, the young woman's father would expect a young man to state his intentions. If he wanted to marry the girl, the two fathers negotiated the dowry (the money and/or property the young woman would bring to the marriage). Those and other details would be put into a marriage contract. Once the contract was signed, the families announced the engagement. The bride-to-be's family hosted a big dinner at their house where the young man gave her an engagement ring.

Now that they were engaged, the young man could visit his fiancée whenever he wanted, but the two young people were always chaperoned. The wedding ceremonies took place at night. Afterward, the bride and groom honeymooned in her parents' home.

Most of these customs have died out over the years, although the practice of asking the father's blessing remains.

Cajun weddings and receptions were, and still are, less formal. It has become a tradition that both of the bride's parents escort her down the aisle. If the wedding is part of a Catholic ceremony, the bride and groom will present a rose to both mothers, and greet their respective parents.

It is Cajun tradition for a newlywed couple to march around the dance floor after entering the reception until everyone has joined in. Then the couple shares in their first dance. If guests want to dance with the bride and groom, they must pin money to the bride's veil or the groom's suit. Guests are encouraged to toast the couple and sing French songs. The wedding dinner features traditional Cajun food, and there are two wedding cakes: one for the bride and a chocolate cake for the groom. It used to be the groom's grandfather or godfather who would cut the cake. Now it can also be done by a sister or aunt of the groom who is not a member of the wedding party.

Above all, Cajun weddings are joyous affairs. "After the wedding there was a big barge waiting on the bayou," recalled Mrs. Joe Giffault. "Everybody danced on the barge all the way back to the house, and when they got to the house they danced all night. I had the best time I ever knowed. . . . The party and the eating and the dancing lasted all night and all the next day."[1]

A contemporary Cajun groom shows the money pinned to his wedding garb by women who wish to dance with him.

Creole society had strict rules for the mourning period following the death of a loved one. The family could not wear jewelry or clothes that were white or brightly colored for six months.

But one unique tradition crossed ethnic and cultural boundaries—the jazz funeral, which dates back at least 200 years with its roots even further back in Africa. It starts with a procession of family and friends walking next to the hearse, accompanied by a jazz band. As noted music historian Eileen Southern notes, "On the way to the cemetery it was customary to play very slowly

The Black Men of Labor band leads the funeral procession of jazz pioneer Ernest "Doc" Paulin into St. Joseph Cemetery in 2007.

and mournfully a dirge, or an 'old Negro spiritual' such as 'Nearer My God to Thee,' but on the return from the cemetery, the band would strike up a rousing, 'When the Saints Go Marching In,' or a ragtime song such as 'Didn't He Ramble.'"[2] At this point, it's common for members of the funeral party to be joined by the "second line," onlookers who join in celebrating the life of the deceased. "Second lining" is a combination of walking and dancing, often accompanied by participants twirling a parasol or handkerchief in the air.

Faubourg Tremé

New Orleans' Tremé district, or Faubourg Tremé, is considered the oldest black neighborhood in America and the birthplace of jazz.

In the years following the Louisiana Purchase, Faubourg Tremé was home to a large, creative, and prosperous community of free black people, although whites and other ethnic groups also lived there. Music flourished in Tremé as did political activism. The local newspaper, *The Tribune*, advocated for African-Americans' civil rights, including the right to vote, to be treated equally under the law, and during the Civil War to have the right to enlist in the Union army.

During Reconstruction after the Civil War, states throughout the south instituted segregation, a blatant infringement of civil rights that would last for nearly a century until the Supreme Court outlawed the practice during the 1950s. During this time of lynchings, Ku Klux Klan raids, and the disintegration of Creole society, a new style of music was born in Faubourg Tremé: jazz, through which black musicians expressed their anger, sorrow, and hope.

Tremé was a center of civil rights activism in the 1950s and '60s. But as the struggle for desegregation succeeded, the more prosperous residents moved out and Tremé became an impoverished neighborhood. It also became known by its official name: the Sixth Ward, which suffered severe damage during Hurricane Katrina in 2005.

The HBO series *Treme*, set in the months and years after Katrina, ran for four seasons. It brought the neighborhood's musical heritage and importance to New Orleans culture to life and showed the Creoles' rich musical legacy that informs jazz and the blues.

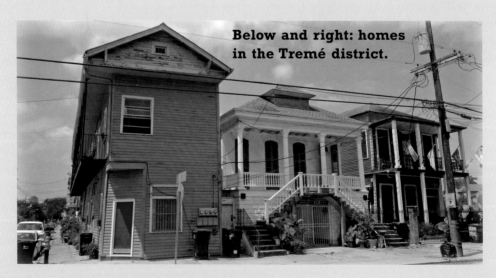

Below and right: homes in the Tremé district.

CHAPTER FIVE
Religious Traditions

For the most part, Cajuns were traditional Catholics who followed Church teachings and maintained fairly conservative social values. The Catholic Creoles saw religion through a more social, proactive context. They showed a special devotion to the Virgin Mary and a devout observance of religious holy days, and holidays, such as All Saints' Day (November 1) and Holy Week leading to Easter. For example, on All Saints' Day Creoles bring flowers made of white, black, or purple tissue paper to place on graves in the cemetery. A week prior to the holiday Creole-run shops display crowns and crosses with black beads.

One of the most famous festivals in the world, Mardi Gras, grew out of Creole religious devotion. According to historians, the roots of Mardi Gras date back thousands of years to various pagan celebrations, especially the Roman festival of Saturnalia. As Christianity spread throughout the Roman Empire, religious leaders integrated this and other popular local traditions into the new faith.

Mardi Gras Parade, New Orleans, Louisiana, 2011

The festival season became a lead-up to Lent, the 40 days of penance and introspection between Ash Wednesday and Easter Sunday. And as Christianity continued to spread, so did the practice of celebrating before Lent. Revelers would gorge on all the meat and dairy products in their homes in preparation for Lent, when they would be prohibited from eating meat and were required to fast. In France, the day before Ash Wednesday came to be known as *Mardi Gras*, or "Fat Tuesday" in English. The word *carnival*, the term used for the pre-Lenten festivities in Hispanic countries, may also refer to the last binge before Lent because the Latin word *carnelevarium* means "to take away or remove meat."

It is believed that the first Mardi Gras celebration in America took place on March 3, 1699, near New Orleans when the French explorers Pierre d'Iberville and Jean-Baptiste de Bienville held a small celebration at a site they named Point du Mardi Gras. By the 1730s, Mardi Gras was celebrated openly in New Orleans, with street parties, masked balls, and sumptuous dinners. The Spanish banned the celebrations when they assumed control of New Orleans. The revelry resumed when Louisiana became a US state in 1812.

During Mardi Gras in 1827, a group of students wearing colorful costumes danced through the streets of New Orleans. Their impromptu parade eventually led to the first recorded New Orleans Mardi Gras parade a decade later. Today, parades of all sizes take place almost daily in New Orleans in the weeks leading up to Mardi Gras. Other enduring traditions include throwing beads and other trinkets, wearing masks, decorating floats, and eating King Cake—cinnamon-filled dough in the shape of a circle which may contain a small plastic figurine representing the baby Jesus.

Mardi Gras celebrations aren't limited to New Orleans. Numerous smaller cities and towns throughout Louisiana also mark the occasion. And cities throughout the rest of the country hold their own observances. The Brazilian city of Rio de Janeiro hosts what may be the world's largest and most elaborate Carnival celebrations.

Thousands of spectators watch the 1906 Rex Krewe Parade on Canal Street. The parade was part of Mardi Gras celebrations.

Voodoo

While the Catholicism observed by Creoles and Cajuns is well-known, lesser known and rarely understood is the belief in voodoo.

Louisiana Voodoo, also known as New Orleans Voodoo, is a cultural form of the Afro-American religions that developed within Louisiana's French, Spanish, and Creole-speaking African Americans. Louisiana Voodoo is often confused with Haitian Voodoo. While the two practices are related, they are distinct from one another.

Louisiana Voodoo is a belief system that combines elements of Catholicism with European and African beliefs. For many generations it was passed from one generation to the next through stories because it does not have a holy book the way the major religions do. As a result, the beliefs of Louisiana Voodoo vary somewhat from person to person.

The word voodoo comes from the African word *vudu*, which refers to a spirit or invisible mysterious force that can intervene in human affairs. By the late 19th and early 20th centuries, outsiders viewed Louisiana Voodoo as witchcraft, and it erroneously became equated with black magic instead of a religious belief system. But followers of Louisiana Voodoo believe in one God and multiple lesser but powerful spirits that preside over daily life issues such as relationships, health, finances, and romance. Voodoo is typically used to cure anxiety, addictions, depression, loneliness, and other physical and emotional ailments. Deceased ancestors can also intercede in the lives of voodoo followers.

"The main focus of Louisiana Voodoo today is to serve others and influence the outcome of life events through the connection with nature, spirits, and ancestors," according to a modern-day Voodoo website. "Voodoo methods include readings, spiritual baths, specially devised diets, prayer, and personal ceremony."[1] Other methods of connecting with spirits include dancing, singing, and other forms of music. Voodoo practitioners may also handle snakes, which symbolize the knowledge of healing and a link between Heaven and Earth.

Voodoo spiritual temple, New Orleans

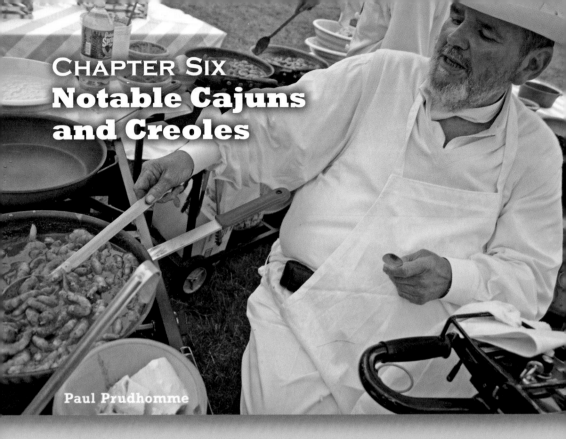

Paul Prudhomme

CHAPTER SIX
Notable Cajuns and Creoles

Paul Prudhomme (1940–)

A Cajun born near New Orleans, chef Paul Prudhomme has made a career out of presenting his take on classic Creole and Cajun dishes. The youngest of 13 children, Prudhomme grew up helping his mother cook. When he was only 17, he got married and opened a hamburger place called Big Daddy-O's Patio. As New Orleans journalist Brett Anderson notes, "Save for the fact that Prudhomme ground his own meat to ensure each hamburger contained the 'proper amount of fat for moisture,' nothing about Big Daddy-O's suggested that its owner would one day become the most famous American restaurant chef in the world. Less than a year after the burger joint's opening, Prudhomme recalled, 'I was out of business. . . . It was a quick nine months.' His marriage was over as well."[1]

He sold magazines for a while before deciding that cooking was what he really wanted to do. After years of traveling to expand his culinary horizons, Prudhomme opened his first restaurant, K-Paul's Louisiana Kitchen, in New Orleans during July 1979. Five years later, he wrote the first of his eight cookbooks. Titled *Chef Paul Prudhomme's Louisiana Kitchen*, it is still considered a classic. He later created a line of all-natural herbs and spices.

Joseph Broussard (1702–1765)

Broussard was born in Port Royal (in modern-day Nova Scotia) in 1702. He settled in what is now New Brunswick with his wife, Agnes, and eventually had eleven children. In the 1720s, he joined in several skirmishes against the British. In the 1740s and 1750s, Broussard was involved in organized armed resistance to British rule. He participated in several wide-ranging campaigns that became increasingly brutal.

He assumed command of Acadian forces following the start of the expulsion in 1755 and led several assaults between then and 1758, when he was seriously wounded. Broussard was captured by the British in 1762 and imprisoned. When he was released two years later, he led a group of Acadians to the Caribbean island of Dominica. When they couldn't adapt to the climate, they sailed to Louisiana early in 1765 and became the first Acadians to settle there. Broussard died several months later. The town of Broussard, Louisiana, is named for Valsin Broussard, one of his direct descendants.

Marie Laveau (1794–1881)

Marie Laveau was a Louisiana Creole who became New Orleans' most famous voodoo priestess. She was the result of a plaçage between a wealthy French planter and a free woman of color. In turn, she had a plaçage that resulted in 15 children. They included her daughter, Marie Laveau II (1827–1895), who also practiced voodoo and amassed a huge following.

Like other Creoles, Laveau was a devout Catholic who attended Mass daily. She added elements of the Catholic religion into voodoo, including statues and saints, prayers and holy water. She had no shortage of customers as news of her ability spread throughout the region. She had been trained as a hairdresser but

This 1920 painting of Marie Laveau by Frank Schneider is based on an 1835 work by George Gatlin.

became famous for telling fortunes and for providing potions and spells, particularly for romantic and financial problems.

Later in life Laveau worked as a nurse during outbreaks of yellow fever and cholera. Her knowledge of the healing qualities of local herbs helped her treat many patients via medicine instead of voodoo.

To many people in New Orleans, she was what might be called today a "civic treasure." As a local newspaper wrote when she died, "All in all Marie Laveau was a most wonderful woman. Doing good for the sake of doing good alone, she obtained no reward, oft times meeting with prejudice and loathing, she was nevertheless contented and did not lag in her work. She always had the cause of the people at heart and was with them in all things."[2]

Ellen DeGeneres (1958–)

Noted TV and film personality Ellen DeGeneres can trace her ancestry back to a French planter who fled the slave uprising in St. Domingue in 1791 and eventually settled in Louisiana. She was born and raised in Metairie, Louisiana, a large suburb of New Orleans. Her parents divorced when she was in her early teens. DeGeneres used humor to cope with the situation. "I was helping [my mother] cope with a broken heart. It brought us closer together and made me realize the power of humor,"[3] she explains.

DeGeneres spent one semester in college before deciding to see if she could make a living as a standup comic. She worked as a clerk in a law firm, a waitress, a bartender, a salesperson, and a house painter to earn money. By the early 1980s she had become popular enough to quit her other jobs and began touring the country. In 1984 the cable network Showtime called her "the funniest person in America." Two years later she became the first female comedian to be invited by Johnny Carson on the *Tonight Show*. Today she is best-known for starring in the 1990s sitcom *Ellen*, serving as the voice of Dory in *Finding Nemo*, and especially for hosting her afternoon talk show, which has won 36 daytime Emmy Awards. In 2014 she acted as the master of ceremonies of

Ellen DeGeneres addresses the Academy Awards on March 21, 2014. It was her second time as host of the ceremonies. The first was in 2007.

the Academy Awards for the second time. During the program, she organized a selfie with about a dozen celebrities that became the most retweeted image in history.

Hunter Hayes (1991–)

Country singer Hunter Hayes was born in Breaux Bridge, Louisiana, to a family that was proud of its Cajun heritage. One of Hunter's babysitters was a fan of famous Cajun accordionist Aldus Roger and played his records all the time. He also loved listening to Cajun songs on the radio. "By the time I was almost two, I was picking up everything and making an instrument out of it,"[4] Hunter recalls. Hayes enjoyed the music so much his grandmother bought him a toy accordion for his second birthday. Three years later, he was playing a custom-made accordion designed for his small hands. He became a local celebrity and started performing with Cajun bands at a nearby restaurant.

In 2000 when he was 10, the regional label Louisiana Red Hot Records released *De Mes Yeux: Through My Eyes*, Hunter's CD of well-known Cajun songs as well as songs he had written. The following year he released his second album, *Make a Wish*.

As a teenager, Hunter played keyboards, guitar, mandolin, and percussion. He put together a home recording studio and taught himself the basics of making records. He moved to Nashville in 2009 when he was 18 and signed a songwriting deal with Universal Music Publishing Group. Two years later, he released his first single, "Storm Warning." He wrote the song and played all the instruments on the track.

His self-titled album debuted in October 2011 and went quadruple-platinum. He earned four Grammy nominations, including Best New Artist. His single "I Want Crazy" was nominated for Best Country Solo Performance. Three years later, he set a Guinness World Record by playing 10 concerts in 10 cities in 24 hours, to benefit the Child Hunger Ends Here program.

Hunter notes, "I've been lucky as a kid. I've met some of the greats, and whether it's Johnny and June (Cash), Charlie Daniels or

Brad Paisley, you could sense they were in it for the love of the music. That was the thing I took away from every single one of those people."[5]

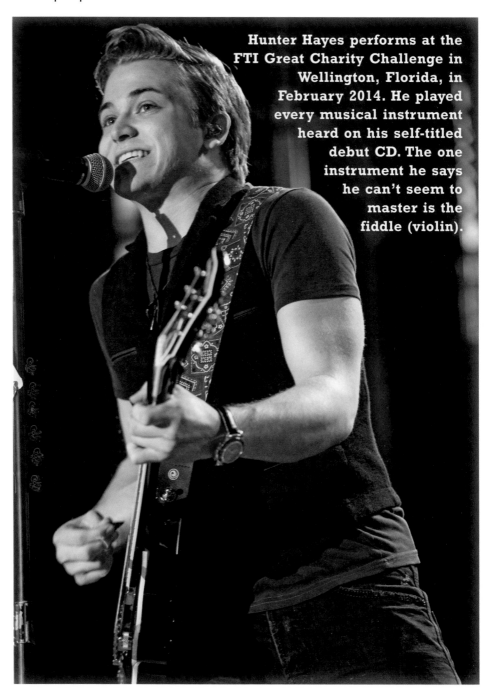

Hunter Hayes performs at the FTI Great Charity Challenge in Wellington, Florida, in February 2014. He played every musical instrument heard on his self-titled debut CD. The one instrument he says he can't seem to master is the fiddle (violin).

Map of Louisiana

■ **The traditional 22 parishes of "Cajun country" or "Acadiana" in southern Louisiana.**

Experiencing Cajun and Creole Culture

Many cities in the United States celebrate Mardi Gras in February or early March. No city tops New Orleans in the scope of its celebrations, which can last for up to two weeks. Well over a million people from all over the United States come to New Orleans for revelry that includes parades with elaborately decorated floats and marching bands, masked balls, throwing beads and other trinkets, and lavish dinners that showcase Cajun and Creole foods.

The second-largest celebration takes place in Mobile, Alabama, where crowds now approach the million mark. Galveston, Texas, and San Diego, California, also host notable Mardi Gras parties. St. Louis, Missouri, has three major Mardi Gras parades, including a pet parade with more than 6,000 animals. "Even tiny Norman,

A Mardi Gras parade float in Lake Charles, LA

Oklahoma, has gotten into the act, spurred on by a homegrown group of women dubbed the Norman Okra Queens," notes *USA Today*. "'We're large and green,' says member Harriette Leigh Kemp."[1]

Likewise, many cities have Cajun and Creole influenced restaurants that serve traditional foods such as gumbo and jambalaya.

The New Orleans Jazz & Heritage Festival, also known as Jazz Fest, is a 10-day cultural event celebrating the history of the region that takes place on the last weekend in April and the first weekend in May every year. Thousands of musicians, chefs, and craftspeople welcome 400,000 visitors who descend on New Orleans.

Many other regions in Louisiana have festivals celebrating Cajun and Creole culture. Lafayette hosts both the Cajun Heartland State Fair in late May and the Cajun and Creole Christmas in December, Jeanerette holds the Creole Festival in April, and Mamou stages the Cajun Music Festival in September.

Musician George Porter, Jr., performs during the New Orleans Jazz & Heritage Festival, better known as Jazz Fest.

TIMELINE

1604	Acadia is founded by French settlers.
1629	Great Britain sends Scottish settlers to Acadia, which is renamed Nova Scotia.
1654	War between Great Britain and France puts Acadia under British rule.
1692	Treaty of Ryswick extends official control of Acadia to France.
1713	The Treaty of Utrecht cedes Acadia to the British.
1718	The city of New Orleans is founded.
1755	Acadians are expelled from Nova Scotia.
1762	The Treaty of Fontainebleu secretly relinquishes Louisiana to Spain.
1765	The first Acadians arrive in Louisiana.
1776	United States declares its independence from Great Britain.
1785	Final mass migration to Louisiana by Acadians exiled in Europe.
1789	French revolution prompts influx of French immigrants to Louisiana.
1791	Slave revolt in Haiti brings more than 10,000 Creoles to Louisiana.
1800	Spain signs Louisiana over to France.
1803	Napoleon Bonaparte sells Louisiana to the United States for $15 million.
1812	Louisiana becomes the 18th state in the Union.
1843	Alexander Mouton is elected the first Acadian governor of Louisiana.
1867	Cajuns establish the first shrimp-canning operation.
1921	Louisiana Constitution prohibits the use of French in the school system.
1928	Joe Falcon and Cléoma Breaux make first recording of a Cajun song.
1968	Council for the Development of French Louisiana (CODOFIL) is created.
1971	Edwin Edwards elected as the first French-speaking governor of Louisiana in the 20th century.
1974	First Acadian music festival is held in Lafayette.
1976	Author Revon Reed publishes *Lâche pas la patate*, the first book in Cajun-French.
1977	The first Cajun French course is offered at Louisiana State University.
1980	US District Court declares Cajuns a minority protected by the Civil Rights Act.
1981	The first Zydeco Festival takes place in St. Landry Parish.
1988	The Louisiana Creole Heritage Center opens at Northwestern State University.
2005	Hurricane Katrina damages many historical sites and decimates the Tremé district.
2014	The Louisiana Cajun-Zydeco Festival moves to Armstrong Park in Tremé.

CHAPTER NOTES

Chapter 1. The Louisiana Purchase

1. Robert W. Tucker and David C. Hendrickson, *Empire of Liberty: The Statecraft of Thomas Jefferson* (New York: Oxford University Press, 1990), p. 164.
2. The Louisiana Purchase Legislative Timeline, Library of Congress. http://memory.loc.gov/ammem/amlaw/louisiana2.html
3. "Letter to John B. Colvin," Thomas Jefferson. Teaching American History, teachingamericanhistory. org/library/document/letter-to-john-b-colvin/
4. "Empire upon the Trails." "The West," PBS. www.pbs.org/weta/thewest/program/episodes/two/index.htm

Chapter 2. The Evolution of the Cajuns

1. 1820 United States census. www.census.gov/prod/www/decennial.html
2. "The Legacy of Cajuns," The Acadians in Louisiana. http://www.vrml.k12.la.us/8th/8_ss/ss_curr/unit5/cajunquiz1/cajuns.htm
3. Carl Brasseaux, *The Founding of New Acadia* (Baton Rouge, LA: Louisiana State University Press, 1997), p. 74.

Chapter 3. The Creoles

1. Helen Bush Caver and Mary T. Williams. "Creoles," Countries and Their Cultures. http://www.everyculture.com/multi/Bu-Dr/Creoles.html

Chapter 4. Traditions

1. Lyle Saxon, *Gumbo Ya-ya: A Collection of Louisiana Folk Tales* (Gretna, LA: Pelican Publishing, 1987), pp. 185–186.

2. "The Jazz Funeral," Neworleansonline.com. http://www.neworleansonline.com/neworleans/multicultural/multiculturaltraditions/jazzfuneral.html

Chapter 5. Religious Traditions

1. "Religion," Marie Laveau's House of Voodoo. http://www.voodooneworleans.com/religion.php

Chapter 6. Notable Cajuns and Creoles

1. Brett Anderson, "Paul Prudhomme: An introduction to an American culinary legend." *The New Orleans Times-Picayune*, June 12, 2005. http://www.nola.com/dining/index.ssf/2005/06/paul_prudhomme.html
2. "Marie Laveau," voodooonthebayou.com. http://www.voodooonthebayou.net/marie_laveau.html
3. "Ellen DeGeneres Biography," People.com. http://www.people.com/people/ellen_degeneres/biography/
4. "About Hunter Hayes," CMT Artists. www.cmt.com/artists/hunter-hayes/biography/
5. Ibid.

Experiencing Cajun and Creole Culture

1. Jayne Clark, "New Orleans has competition for Mardi Gras." *USA Today*, February 17, 2006. http://usatoday30.usatoday.com/travel/destinations/2006-02-17-mardi-gras_x.htm?POE=TRVISVA

FURTHER READING

Books

KidsCap. *The Louisiana Purchase: A History Just for Kids*. Anaheim, CA: Golgotha Press, 2012.

Landau, Elaine. *The Louisiana Purchase: Would You Close the Deal* (What Would You Do?). Berkeley Heights, NJ: Enslow, 2010.

Macaulay, Ellen. *Louisiana* (From Sea to Shining Sea). Danbury, CT: Children's Press, 2009.

Murray, Julie. *Mardi Gras*. Pinehurst, NC: Buddy Books, 2014.

Person, Stephen. *Voodoo in New Orleans*, New York, NY: Bearport Publishing, 2010.

Works Consulted

Ancelet, Barry Jean. *Cajun and Creole Music Makers*. Jackson, MS: University of Mississippi Press, 1999.

Anderson, Brett. "Paul Prudhomme: An introduction to an American culinary legend." *The New Orleans Times-Picayune*, June 12, 2005. http://www.nola.com/dining/index.ssf/2005/06/paul_prudhomme.html

Bernard, Shane K. *The Cajuns: Americanization of a People*. Jackson, MS: University of Mississippi Press, 2003.

Bienvenue, Marcelle, Carl Brasseaux and Ryan Brasseaux. *Stir the Pot: A History of Cajun Cuisine*. New York: Hippocrene Books, 2005.

Brasseaux, Carl. *The Founding of New Acadia*. Baton Rouge, LA: Louisiana State University Press, 1997.

Caver, Helen Bush, and Mary T. Williams. "Creoles," Countries and Their Cultures. http://www.everyculture.com/multi/Bu-Dr/Creoles.html

Clark, Jayne. "New Orleans has competition for Mardi Gras." *USA Today*, February 17, 2006. http://usatoday30.usatoday.com/travel/destinations/2006-02-17-mardi-gras_x.htm?POE=TRVISVA

Conrad, Glenn R., ed. *The Cajuns: Essays on Their History and Culture*. Lafayette, LA: Center for Louisiana Studies, University of Southwestern Louisiana, 1983.

Dorman, James H. *The People Called Cajuns*. Lafayette, LA: Center for Louisiana Studies, University of Southwestern Louisiana, 1983.

"Ellen DeGeneres Biography," People.com http://www.people.com/people/ellen_degeneres/biography/

FrenchCreoles.com www.frenchcreoles.com

FURTHER READING

"The Jazz Funeral." Neworleansonline.com.
http://www.neworleansonline.com/neworleans/multicultural/
multiculturaltraditions/jazzfuneral.html

Jefferson, Thomas. "Letter to John B. Colvin." Teaching American
History. teachingamericanhistory.org/library/document/letter-to-
john-b-colvin/

Kein, Sybil. *Creole: The History and Legacy of Louisiana's Free People of
Color*. Baton Rouge, LA: Louisiana State University Press, 2009.

LaBorde, Judy. "A Short History of the Acadians and Cajuns." Genetics
and Louisiana Families, LSU Health Sciences Center.
http://www.medschool.lsuhsc.edu/genetics_center/louisiana/
article_cajunhistory.htm

The Louisiana Purchase Legislative Timeline, Library of Congress.
http://memory.loc.gov/ammem/amlaw/louisiana2.html

"Mardi Gras." History Channel
www.history.com/topics/mardi-gras

Marie Laveau," voodooonthebayou.com
http://www.voodooonthebayou.net/marie_laveau.html

Richard, Zachary. *The History of the Acadians of Louisiana*. Lafayette,
LA: University of Louisiana at Lafayette, 2013.

"Roots of Cajun Culture." Louisiana Travel
www.louisianatravel.com/roots-cajun-culture

Rushton, William Faulkner. *The Cajuns: From Acadia to Louisiana*. New
York: Farrar, Straus & Giroux, 1979.

Savoy, Ann Allen. *Cajun Music: A Reflection of a People*. Eunice, LA:
Bluebird Press, 1984.

Saxon, Lyle. *Gumbo Ya-ya: A Collection of Louisiana Folk Tales*. Gretna,
LA: Pelican Publishing, 1987.

Tidwell, Michael. *Bayou Farewell: The Rich Life and Tragic Death of
Louisiana's Cajun Coast*. New York: Vintage Departures, 2003.

Trillin, Calvin. "Missing Links." *The New Yorker*, January 28, 2002.
http://www.newyorker.com/archive/2002/01/28/020128fa_
fact_trillin

Tucker, Robert W., and David C. Hendrickson. *Empire of Liberty: The
Statecraft of Thomas Jefferson*. New York: Oxford University Press,
1990.

GLOSSARY

andouille (ahn-DOO-ee)—A spicy, smoked country sausage.

Cajun (KAY-djun)—Descendants of the people of Nova Scotia who settled in Louisiana.

crawfish (CRAW-fish)—A small crustacean resembling a lobster, known locally as mudbug.

Creole (CREE-ohl)—A descendant of French or Spanish settlers; a person of mixed European and African blood.

gumbo (GUM-boh)—A soup thickened with okra and containing meat and/or seafood and vegetables.

levee (LEH-vee)—An embankment built to keep a river from overflowing; a landing place on the river.

plaçage (plah-KAZH)—A common-law marriage between a white man and a woman of color or mixed race.

voodoo (VOOH-doo)—A Caribbean religion combining elements of Roman Catholicism and African rituals.

zydeco (ZIGH-duh-coh)—A lively blend of French and Caribbean music, often played with guitar, washboard, and accordion.

INDEX

Acadia 16–17
Acadians 18–19, 21
    agriculture 22
    music 32
All Saints' Day 42
Bonaparte, Napoleon 9, 10
Broussard, Joseph 49
Broussard, Valsin 49
Cajuns
    cuisine 33–34
    cultural events 57
    marriage 36
    music 32
    origins 6, 16–19
    religion 42
Canal Street 28
Carson, Johnny 51
Civil War 6, 19, 28, 40
Claiborne, William 27
Creoles
    assimilation 29
    colonial society 26–27
    cuisine 33–34
    cultural events 57
    dancing 32–33
    language 26, 28, 35
    marriage 35–36
    origins 6, 24, 26
    post-Civil War 28
    religion 42
de Bienville, Jean-Baptiste 9
DeGeneres, Ellen 51, 53
de la Salle, Robert 6, 8–9
de Soto, Hernando 6
d'Iberville, Pierre 9
Duke William 18
étouffée 33
French and Indian War 9
French Quarter 28
George II, King 17
gumbo 57
Haiti 30–31

Hayes, Hunter 53–54
Homestead Act 14
jambalaya 34, 57
Jazz Fest 57
jazz funeral 38–39
Jefferson, Thomas 9–12
King Cake 44
Laveau, Marie 49, 51
Laveau II, Marie 49
Lawrence, Charles 17
Lent 44
Livingston, Robert 9, 10
Louis XIV, King 9
Louisiana
    exploration 9
    statehood 6
Louisiana Purchase 8, 10–12
L'Ouverture, Toussaint 31
Manifest Destiny 14
Mardi Gras 42, 44, 56
Mississippi River 8, 9, 10, 18,
    19, 22
Monroe, James 9, 10
Napoleonic Code 6
New Orleans 9, 10, 26, 27, 29, 30,
    40, 44, 51, 56
Nova Scotia 6, 16, 17
plaçages 26
Point du Mardi Gras 44
O'Sullivan, John 14
Prudhomme, Paul 48–49
Republic of West Florida 6
Roger, Aldus 53
Saint-Domingue 30
Saturnalia 42
"second line" 39
Tremé 40
Vendée (region in France) 16
Vertières, Battle of 31
Voodoo 46
World War II 21
zydeco 32

About the Author

Kathleen Tracy has been a journalist and author for more than twenty years. She has traveled extensively throughout her career, traveling throughout Europe, the South Pacific, and Central America. The author also lived in North Africa for two months while researching an article on movie production, spending extensive time in Tunisia and Egypt.